THE BOOK OF THE DEAD

FACSIMILE

OF

THE PAPYRUS

OF

ANI

IN THE BRITISH MUSEUM

Printed by Order of the Trustees

SECOND EDITION

SOLD AT THE BRITISH MUSEUM;
AND BY
LONGMANS & CO., 39, PATERNOSTER ROW; B. QUARITCH, 15, PICCADILLY;
ASHER & CO., 13, BEDFORD STREET, COVENT GARDEN;
KEGAN PAUL, TRENCH, TRÜBNER & CO., LTD., CHARING CROSS ROAD; AND
HENRY FROWDE, OXFORD UNIVERSITY PRESS, AMEN CORNER.

1894.

TABLE OF PLATES.

Plate	1.	Invocation to Rā, with vignette.	Plate	22.	Chap. 135; Chap. 134, with vignette.
„	2.	Vignette representing Sunrise (Book of the Dead, Chap. 16a); Invocation to Osiris, with vignette.	„	23.	Chap. 13, with vignette.
„	3, 4.	Vignette of the Weighing of the Heart (Psychostasia) and of the Introduction of Ani into the presence of Osiris, with text.	„	24.	Chap. 30 (continued); Chap. 125, with vignette.
			„	25.	Chap. 26, with vignette; Chap. 77, with vignette; Chap. 78, with vignette.
„	5.	Book of the Dead, Chap. 1, with vignette.	„	26.	Chap. 78 (continued).
„	6.	Chap. 1 (continued), with vignette; Chap. 22; Rubric of Chap. 72.	„	27.	Chap. 87, with vignette; Chap. 88, with vignette; Chap. 82, with vignette; Chap. 85, with vignette; Chap. 83, with vignette.
„	7–10.	Chap. 17, with vignettes.	„	28.	Chap. 84, with vignette; Chap. 85; Chap. 81 a, with vignette; Chap. 80, with vignette.
„	11, 12.	Chaps. 14[?] and 147, with vignettes; vignettes and texts introductory to Chap. 18.			
„	13, 14.	Chap. 18, with vignettes.	„	29.	Chap. 175, with vignette.
„	15.	Chap. 23; Chap. 24; Chap. 26, with vignette; Chap. 30a; Chap. 61, with vignette; Chap. 54, with vignette; Chap. 29, with vignette; Chap. 27.	„	30.	Chapter Introductory to the Negative Confession (Chap. 125); Vignette of Osiris and Isis within a Shrine.
			„	31.	The Negative Confession, with vignettes.
„	16.	Chap. 27 (continued), with vignette; Chap. 58, with vignette; Chap. 59, with vignette; Chap. 44, with vignette; Chap. 45, with vignette; Chap. 46, with vignette; Chap. 50, with vignette.	„	32.	Negative Confession (continued), with vignettes; Table of Parts of the Body and the gods to whom they are assimilated (from Chap. 42).
			„	33.	Rubric of Chap. 42 or 125, and vignette of Chap. 126; Chap. 133, with vignette; Chap. 136, with vignette; Chap. 100, with vignette; Chap. 146, with vignette; Chap. 147, with vignette.
„	17.	Chap. 93, with vignette; Chap. 43, with vignette; Chap. 89, with vignette; Chap. 91, with vignette; Chap. 92, with vignette.			
„	18.	Chap. 92 (continued), with vignette; Chap. 74, with vignette; Chap. 8, with vignette; Chap. 2, with vignette; Chap. 9, with vignette; Chap. 132, with vignette; Chap. 10; Chap. 15.	„	34.	Chap. 151 (continued); Chap. 110.
			„	35.	Vignettes of Chap. 149; Vignette of the Seven Cows and their Bull (Chap. 148); Introductory text and vignette of the deceased in the presence of Rā.
„	19.	Chap. 15 (continued), with vignettes; Vignette representing Ani and his Wife, with their Names and Titles, Litany to Osiris; Hymn to Rā.	„	36.	Vignette of the Four Rudders of the cardinal points and their gods; Invocation to Osiris (Chap. 16[3]).
„	20.	Vignette representing Osiris and Isis within a Shrine; Chap. 18.	„	37.	Vignette of Hekau-Osiris within a Shrine; Chap. 186, and vignette of Hathor (a) in the form of a Hippopotamus, and (b) in that of the Cow Meh-urit issuing from the side of a mountain.
„	21.	Chap. 18 (continued), with vignette; Chap. 125.			

TABLE OF CHAPTERS.

Chapters		Plate
I.	The beginning of the Chapters of "Coming forth by day"	5, 6
II.	The Chapter of coming forth by day [and] of living after death	16
VIII.	The Chapter of passing through the underworld by day	18
IX.	The Chapter of coming forth by day after passing through the hall of the tomb	12
X.	See Chapter XLVIII.	16
XV.	A Hymn of praise to Rā when he riseth in the eastern horizon of the sky	4
XV.	A Hymn of praise to Osiris Unnefer	2
XV.	A Hymn of praise to Rā when he setteth in the land of life	8–11
XVII.	The beginning of the praisings and glorifyings of coming forth and going into the underworld	7–10
XVIII.	Introduction (A and B), text (B A–J), and Rubric. (This chapter has no title.)	13, 14
XVIII.	Duplicate copy, with Rubric	23, 24
XXII.	The Chapter of giving a mouth to Osiris	6
XXIII.	The Chapter of opening the mouth of Osiris	15
XXIV.	The Chapter of bringing enchantments to Osiris	15
XXVI.	The Chapter of giving a heart to Osiris	15
XXVII.	The Chapter of not letting be snatched off the heart of a man from him in the underworld	15
XXIX.	The Chapter of not letting be removed the heart of a man from him in the underworld	15
XXIXA.	The Chapter of a heart of carnelian	15

TABLE OF CHAPTERS.

THE BOOK OF THE DEAD

THE PAPYRUS OF ANI

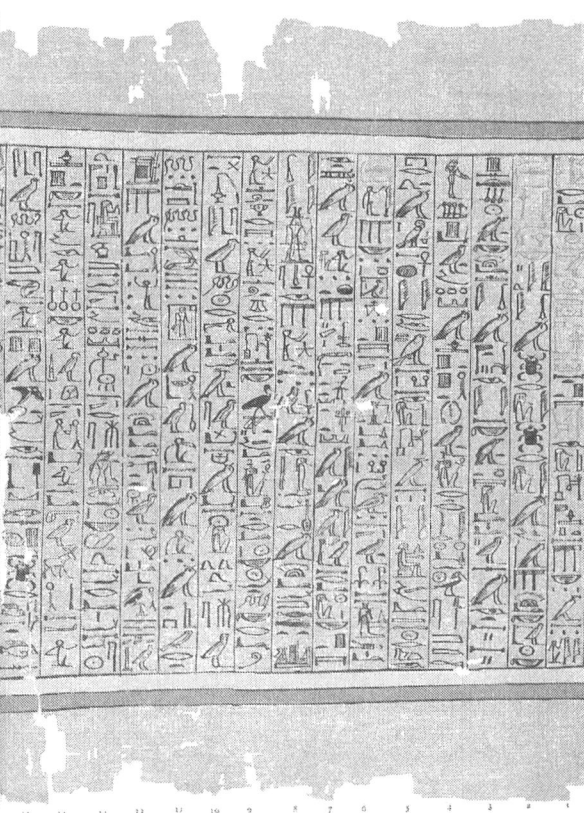

Vignette: Ani, "Scribe of the Sacred Revenues of all the gods of Thebes," and administrator of "the Granaries of the Lords of Abydos," and his wife Thuthu before a table of offerings of meat, cakes, fruit, flowers, etc.

Text: Hymn in honour of the sun-god Rā at his rising.

THE BOOK OF THE DEAD

THE PAPYRUS OF ANI

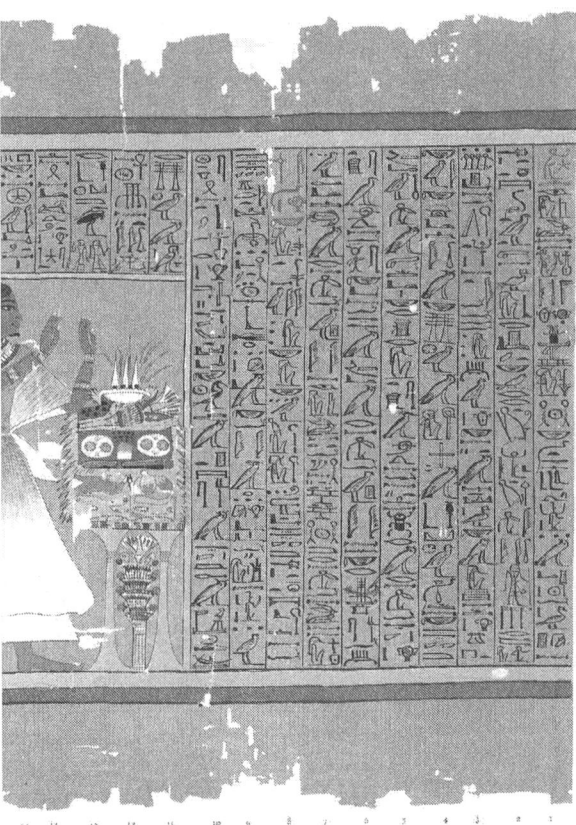

2.—*Vignettes*: (1) Isis and Nephthys, the sisters of Osiris, kneeling in adoration on the left and right of the Tat, a symbol of Osiris, which stands upon the Solar Mount and supports the Sign of Life upholding the Sun-disk. The ornaments upon the heads of the two goddesses are the hieroglyphic signs of their names. On each side, three cynocephali or dog-headed apes, the transformed openers of the eastern portals of heaven, raising their hands in adoration. (2) Ani and his wife before a table of offerings.

Text: Invocation to Osiris.

THE BOOK OF THE DEAD

THE PAPYRUS OF ANI

3.—*Vignette*: Above, twelve gods seated in cadre, as judges, before a table of offerings. Below, the Psychostasia, or Weighing of the Conscience; the jackal-headed Anubis trying in the Balance the heart (conscience) of the deceased against the feather symbolical of Law; on the left, Ani and his wife in an attitude of devotion; on the right, the ibis-headed Thoth, the scribe of the gods, noting down the result of the trial, and behind him the monster *Amemit*, the Devourer. On the left of the balance, Shaï (Destiny) with the two goddesses Rennut and Meschenit behind him; above them, the soul of Ani, as a human-headed hawk, and the symbol of the cradle.

Text: On the left, the address of Ani to his heart; on the right, the sentence of acquittal.

THE BOOK OF THE DEAD

THE PAPYRUS OF ANI

4

4.—*Vignette*: The presentation of Ani, triumphant, to Osiris. The god enthroned within a shrine; behind him, Isis and Nephthys; in front a lotus-flower, on which are the four children of Horus, gods of the dead. On the left, Horus leads forward Ani, who again kneels, with whitened hair, and presents offerings.

Text: The address of Horus to Osiris, announcing the righteousness of Ani; and the prayer of Ani.

THE BOOK OF THE DEAD

CHAP. I

THE PAPYRUS OF ANI 5

Vignette: Funeral procession: the mummy on a boat-shaped hearse, drawn by oxen, beside it kneels the mourning wife; in front, a priest officiates; behind follow mourners, and servants drawing a funereal shrine and bearing articles for the tomb, among which is the deceased's writing palette.

Text: Chapter I of the Book of the Dead.

THE BOOK OF THE DEAD

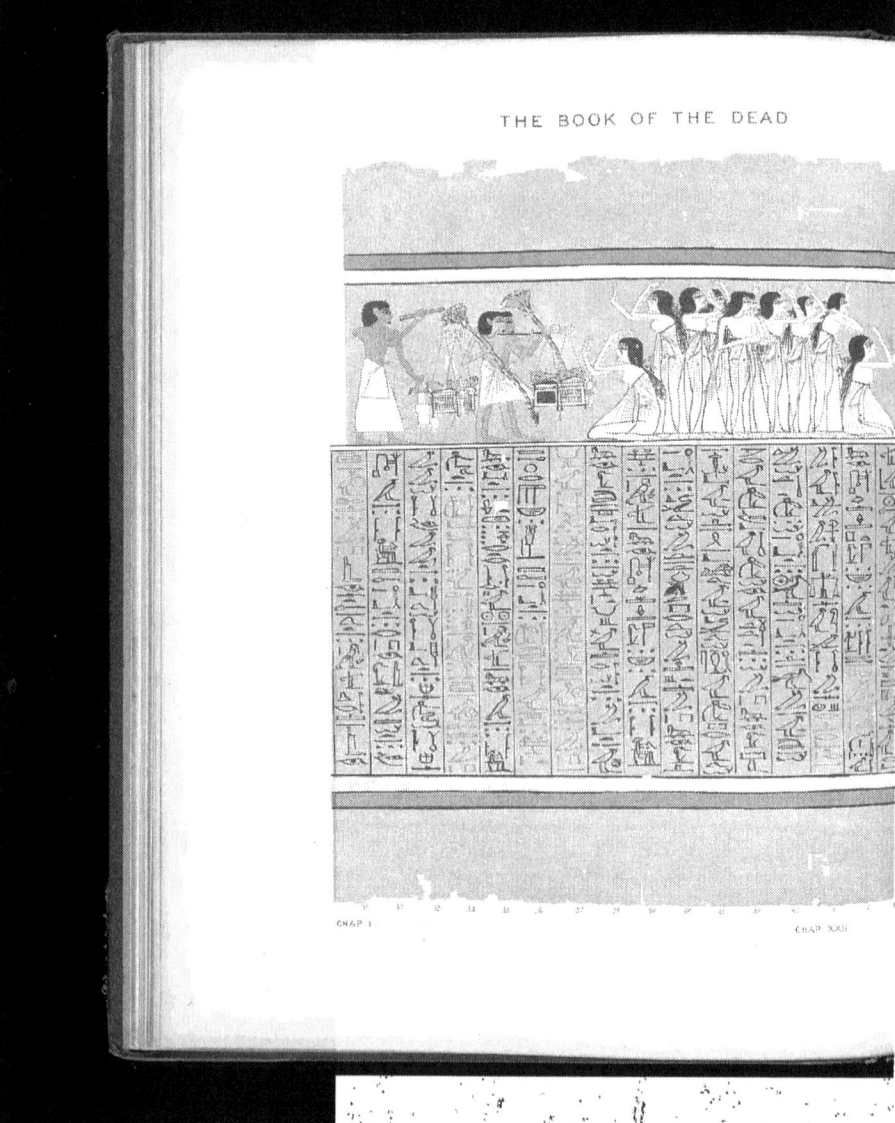

CHAP. I.   CHAP. XXII

THE PAPYRUS OF ANI

RUBRIC OF
CHAP. LXXII.

Lower Vignette: Funeral procession continued; oxen-carts carrying sepulchral furniture; a band of female mourners. On the right, the tomb, in front of which Anubis supports the mummy, the mourning wife kneeling before it. Facing the mummy, two priests officiate before a table of offerings; behind them, a priest reads the funeral service from a papyrus, and a shaven priest brings Kerasef an offering; the cuff and cow above symbolise the rising Sun and Heaven.

Text: Chapter 22, and rubric of the 72nd chapter of the Book of the Dead.

THE BOOK OF THE DEAD

CHAP. XVII

THE PAPYRUS OF ANI

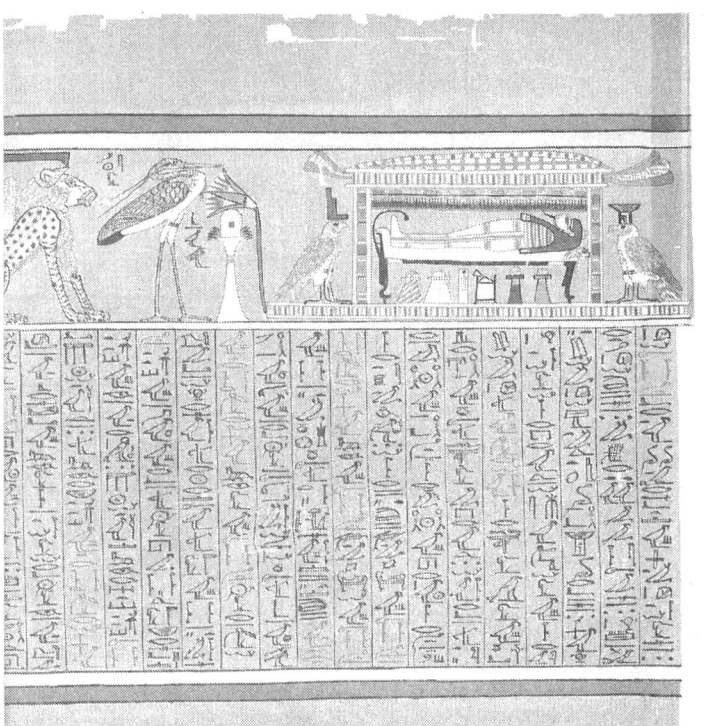

Vignette: (a) Ani, playing at draughts, together with his wife, sitting a hall. (b) Their two souls standing above the tomb, in front of them, on altar with a libation-vase and lotus flowers. (c) The Sparrow-hawk in the solar barque, with the company of heaven above, on either side the lions "Yesterday" and "To-morrow," otherwise Shuti and Sū. (d) The Horus identified with Osiris, an altar with vase and lotus-flower before him. (e) The mummy in a shrine, with Isis and Nephthys in the form of twin birds; beneath the bier are jars, the writing pallet, etc.

Text. Chapter 17, "of the praisings and glorifications of coming forth and entering in the nether-world," etc., of the Book of the Dead.

THE BOOK OF THE DEAD

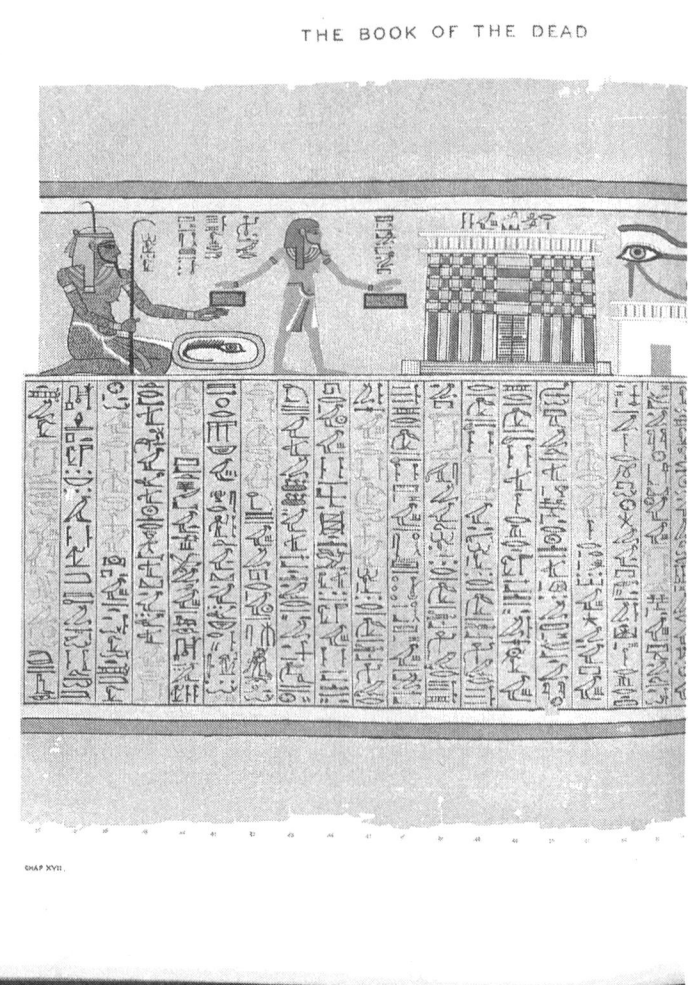

CHAP XVII.

THE PAPYRUS OF ANI

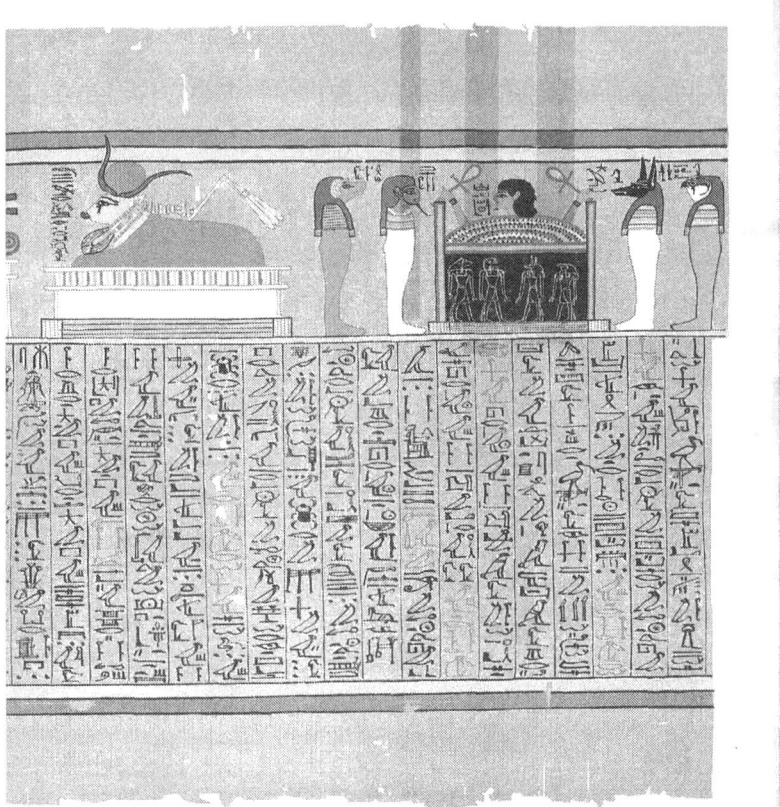

Vignettes: (a) A seated male figure with the emblem of "millions of years" in his right hand and on his head; his left hand extended above the Eye of Horus. (b) A male figure standing with arms outstretched above the Eyes of "Maāti" and "Hormen" (?) attributes. (c) A pylon, or gate, with folding doors; "The Door of the Funeral Passages." (d) The Eye of Horus upon a pedestal. (e) The great cow "Meh-urt, the Eye of Rā." (f) A funeral chest, surrounded by the four children of Horus, with Rā rising from it holding the Sign of Life in each hand.

Text: Chapter 17 (continued) of the Book of the Dead.

THE BOOK OF THE DEAD

CHAP. XVII.

THE PAPYRUS OF ANI

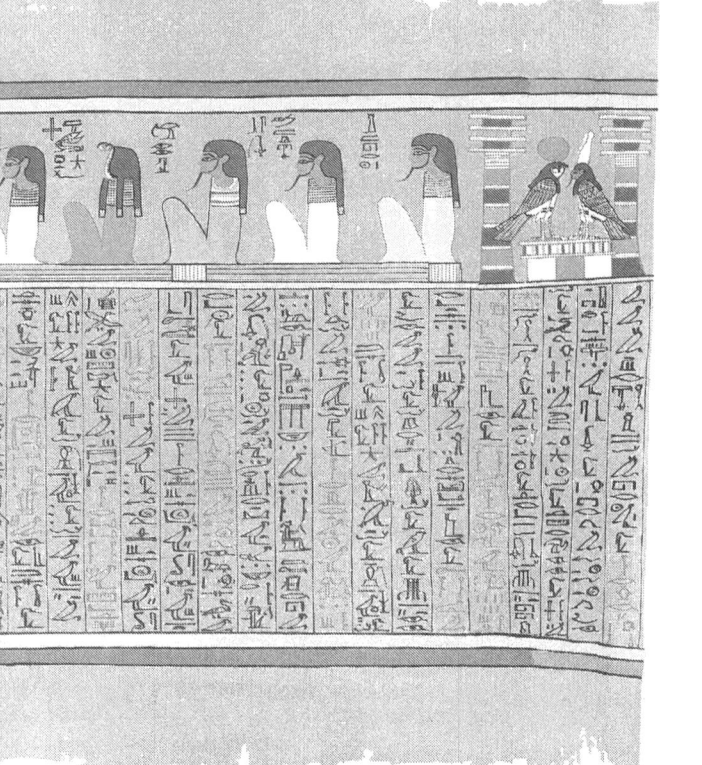

Plate 9. (a) Eleven deities, viz., Maat-ur, Kher-beq-f, Heru, Khent-en-maat, and Anubis, and the seven gods identified with the seven stars of the constellation of the Great Bear. (b) The souls of Rā and Osiris between two Tats signifying their meeting-place Tattu.

Text: Chapter 17 (continued) of the Book of the Dead.

THE BOOK OF THE DEAD

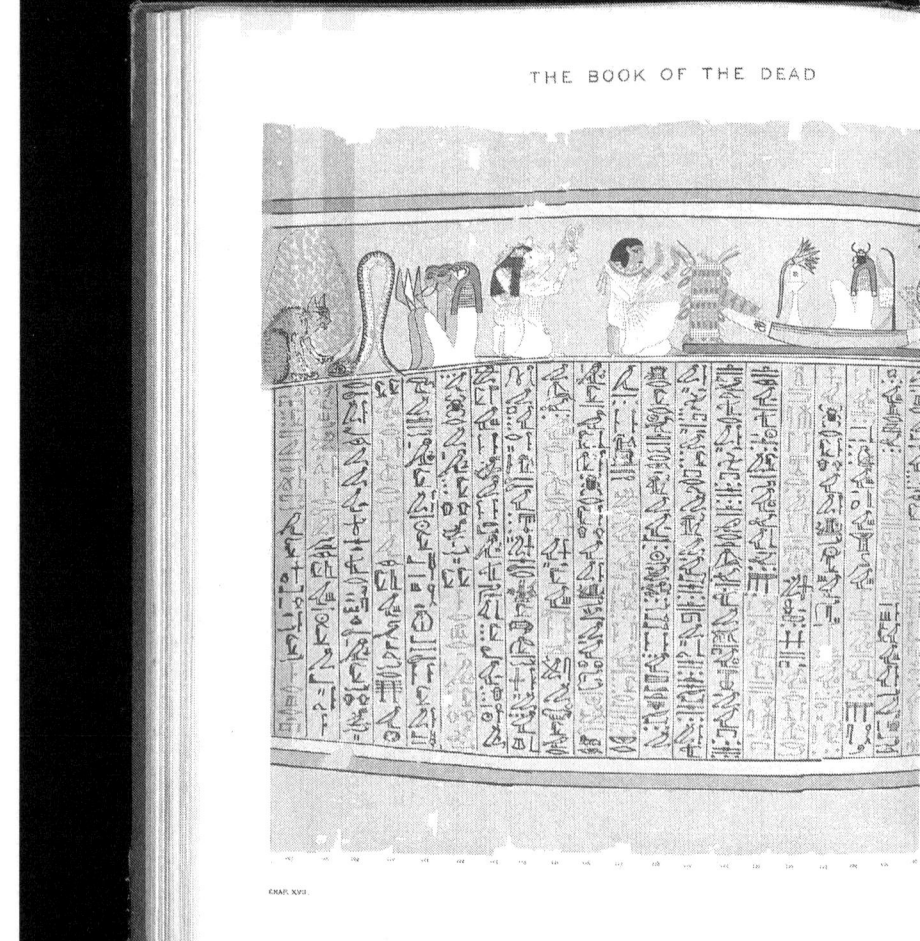

CHAP. XVII.

THE PAPYRUS OF ANI

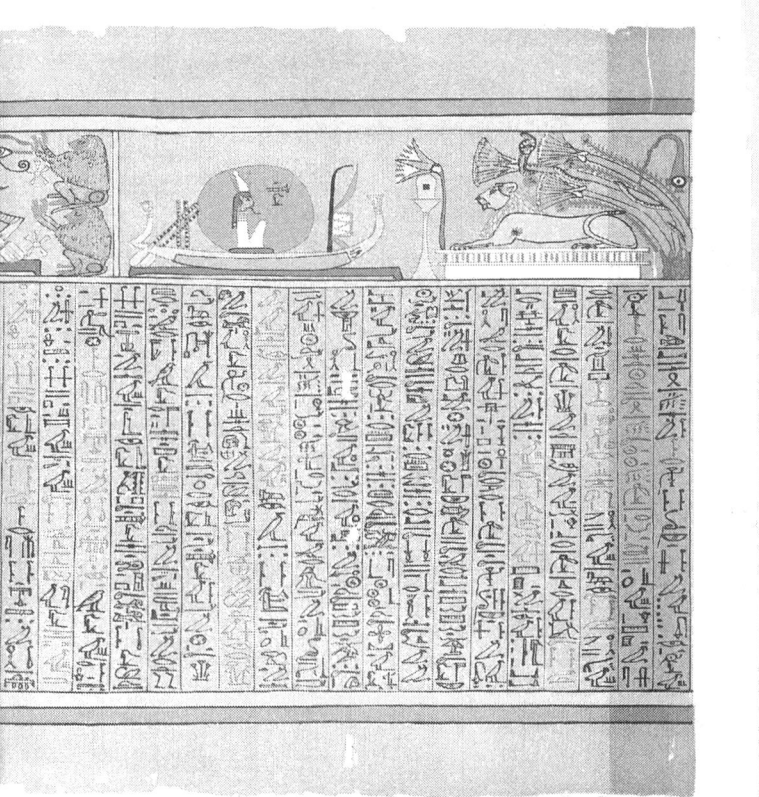

36.—*Vignettes*: (1) A cat in front of a persea tree cutting off the head of a serpent, symbolizing the rising sun-god Ra slaying the dragon of Darkness; the gods Hu, Ani, and their father Tem looking on. (2) Ani and his wife seated on the sacred-breasted god Kheperà, of the morning, who is seated in the solar Bark floating on the heavens with an altar and funeral-stele before them. Two cynocephali, spirits of dawn, with their paws raised in adoration, within the Sun-disk in the Solar Bark, facing an altar with lotus flower. (3) The god Tmu, the closer of the day, seated, within the Sun-disk, in the Solar Bark, facing an altar with lotus flower. (4) A monkey-headed figure, enthroned in lotus flowers, among which is a serpent "Uatchit the Fiery," symbolizing the Dawn and the Plains of Aan.

Text.—Chapter 17 (continued) of the Book of the Dead.

THE PAPYRUS OF ANI

SECOND ĀRIT   THIRD ĀRIT   FOURTH ĀRIT

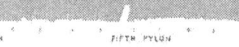

THIRD PYLON   FOURTH PYLON   FIFTH PYLON   SIXTH PYLON

11.—*Vignette*: Ani and his wife approaching (*a*) the seven gates called Ārit and (*b*) the ten Pylons of Osiris (extending into Plate 12). Each of the Ārit gates is guarded by a Doorkeeper, a Watcher, and a Herald; and each of the pylons by a Doorkeeper.

Text: Chapters 146 and 147 of the Book of the Dead; being the names of the guardians of the Ārit gates and pylons, and the addresses made by Ani to these gods.

THE BOOK OF THE DEAD

CHAP. CXLVII continued. FIFTH ĀRIT   SIXTH ĀRIT

CHAP. CXLVI continued. SEVENTH PYLON   EIGHTH PYLON   NINTH PYLON   TENTH PY

THE PAPYRUS OF ANI

11.—*Vignettes*: (*a*) Continuation of the vignettes in Plate 11. (*b*) Ani, (wearing sandals) and his wife, take representatives, preceded by a priest robed in the panther-skin and advancing towards two pylons (see Plate 13).
Text: Chapters 146 and 147 (continued) of the Book of the Dead; and invocations of the priest and of Ani, forming an Introduction to Chapter 18 of the Book of the Dead, which contains the Litany of Thoth.

THE BOOK OF THE DEAD

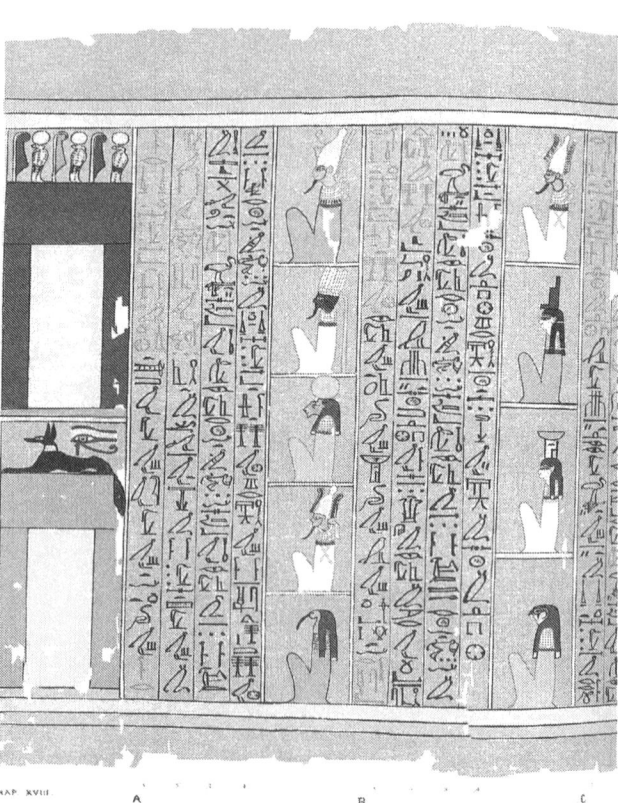

THE PAPYRUS OF ANI

D   E

13.—Vignettes. The nine palms whereby are approached the gods which preside over certain localities, twenty-three of whom are here depicted.
Text: Chapter 18 of the Book of the Dead.

THE BOOK OF THE DEAD

CHAP. XVIII. continued.
F G H

THE PAPYRUS OF ANI   14

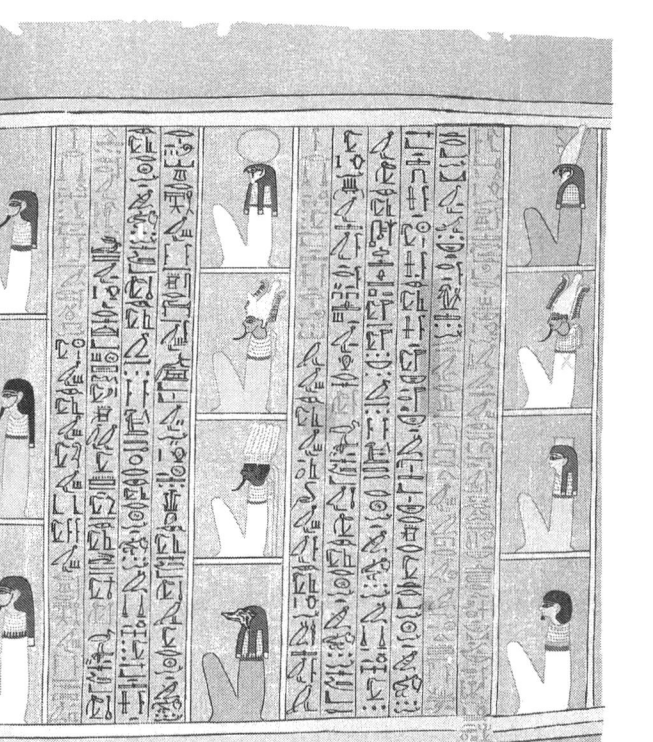

12.—Rubric: Nineteen of the gods of Lamentation (continued from Plate 13)
Text: Chapter 18 (continued) of the Book of the Dead.

THE BOOK OF THE DEAD

CHAP. XXIII. CHAP. XXIV. CHAP. XXVI.

THE PAPYRUS OF ANI

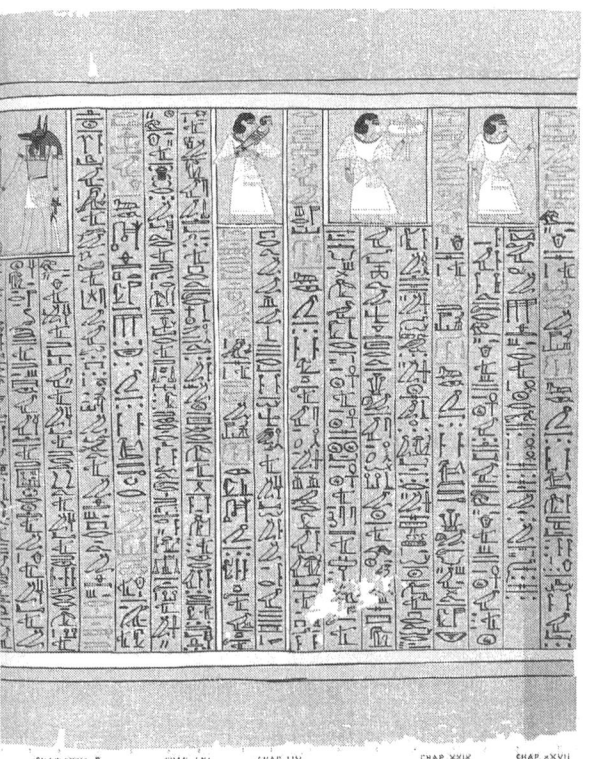

CHAP. XXX B.   CHAP. LXI.   CHAP. LIV.   CHAP. XXIX   CHAP. XXVII

15.—*Vignettes.* (a) A priest raising above the head of Ani the instrument to open his mouth, to illustrate the chapter "of opening the mouth." (b) Ani making an offering to the jackal-headed Am-khe, to illustrate the chapter "of giving his heart to the deceased." (c ?) Ani carrying his soul, to illustrate "that the soul of the deceased may not be taken from him;" carrying an inflated sail, to illustrate the chapter "of giving air" and advancing with a staff.

Text. Chapters 23, 74, 26, 30B, 61, 54, 29, and 27, of the Book of the Dead; opening the mouth, bringing words of power, receiving the heart, and giving air to the deceased, in the nether-world.

THE BOOK OF THE DEAD

THE PAPYRUS OF ANI

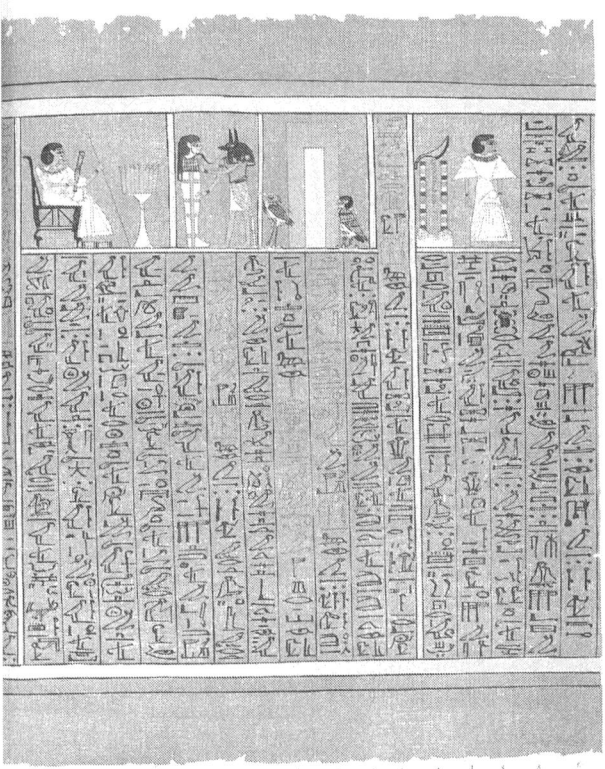

PL XCIV.   CHAP. XLV.   CHAP. XLVI.   CHAP. L.

16.—*Vignettes.* (*a*) Ani, with his heart placed before him, supplicating four gods, to illustrate "that the heart of a person may be taken from him." (*b, c*) Ani and his soul drinking water; and Nu, the goddess of the sky, in the sycamore tree, giving fruit to Ani, to illustrate the chapters "of breathing of air and arresting water." (*d*) Ani seated before an altar, to illustrate the chapter "of not dying the second death." (*e*) Anubis holding the mummy of Ani, to illustrate the chapter "of not turning to corruption." (*f*) A pylon, with a feather and a seal. (*g*) Ani turning from the knife and block, to illustrate the chapter "of not entering into the place of divine execution."

Text. Chapters 27 (continued) 38, 39, 44, 45, 46, 50, and 92, of the Book of the Dead.

THE BOOK OF THE DEAD

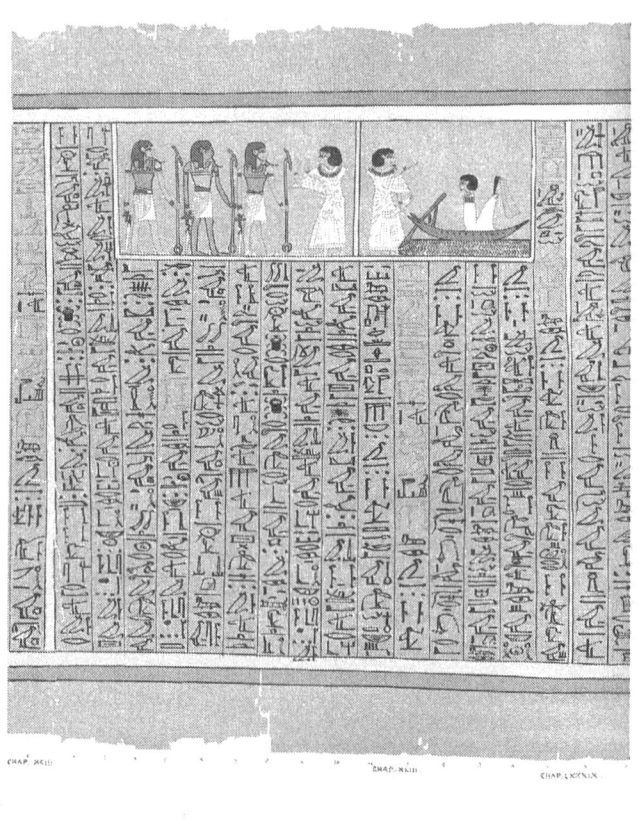

THE PAPYRUS OF ANI 17

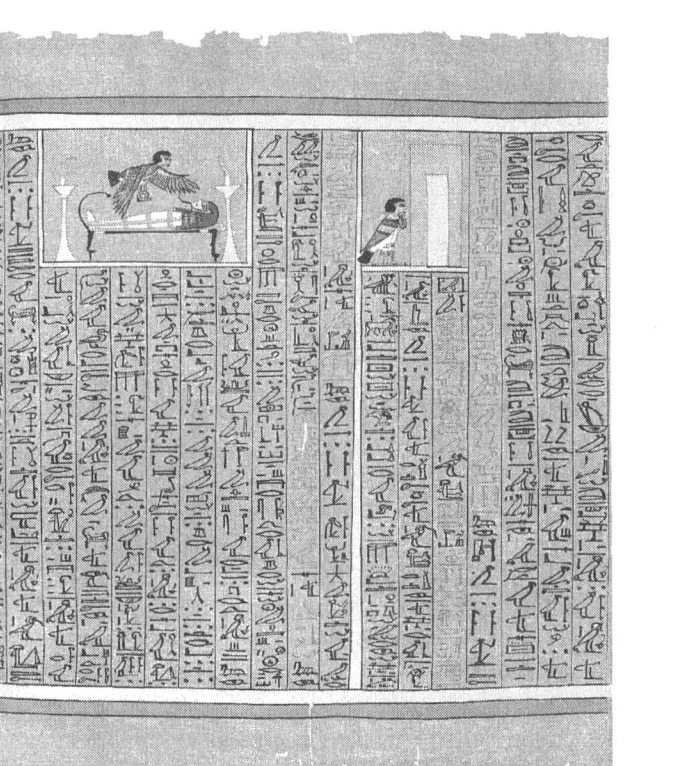

Plate I. *Vignettes:* (a) Ani adoring a triad of gods. (b) Ani, with his writing pallet in his left hand, addressing a god, who with vested head is seated in a boat. (c) The soul of Ani visiting his mummified body, to illustrate the chapter "of re-uniting the soul to the dead body." (d) The soul standing before a door-way, to illustrate the chapter "that the soul of a person may not be imprisoned."

Text. Chapters 23, 43, 89, 91, and 92, of the Book of the Dead.

THE BOOK OF THE DEAD

THE PAPYRUS OF ANI

18

CHAP. IX.   CHAP. CXXXII.   CHAP. X [XLVIII].   CHAP. XV.

18.—*Vignettes*: (a) Ani entering a doorway on the other side of which is his Shadow accompanied by his Soul, to illustrate the chapter "of opening the tomb to the soul and shade." (b) Ani offering before the shrine of the Divine Bark of Châis-Seker. (c) Ani entering Amenta (the netherworld) represented by a hawk and a feather upon a stand upheld by the æther mount, to illustrate the chapter "of approaching Amenta by day." (d) Ani, before an altar with vase and lotus flower, adoring the god Osiris in form of a ram crowned with the triple crown, which is composed of the *uas*-disk and crowns of Upper and Lower Egypt, flanked by the two feathers, or double *Law*; the illustrate the chapter "of coming forth by day after entering the Ameenhet." (e) Ani standing by a doorway, to illustrate the chapter "of the person going round to see his house." (f) Ani slaying a serpent.

Text. Chapters on [missing text] of the Book of the Dead.

THE BOOK OF THE DEAD

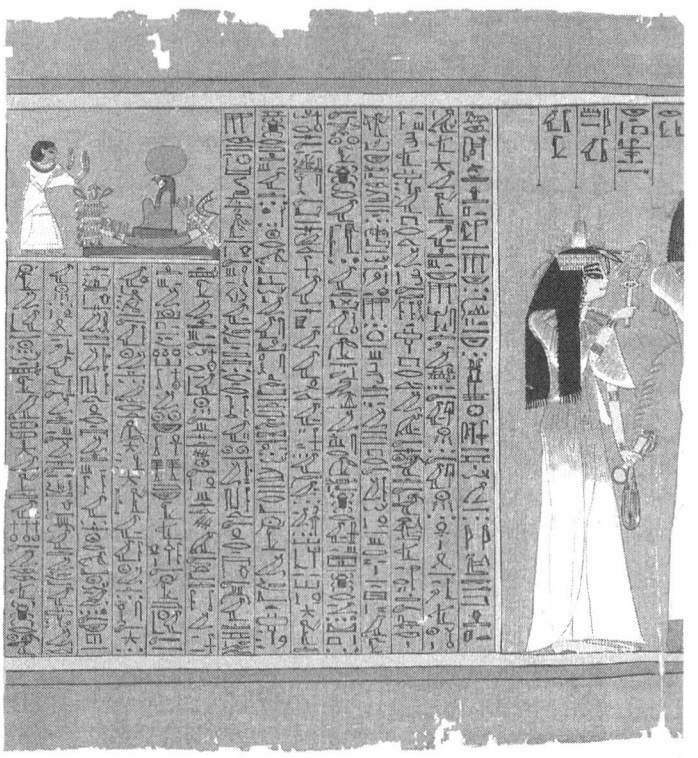

CHAP. XV. continued.

THE PAPYRUS OF ANI

19

LITANY TO OSIRIS   HYMN TO RA

19.—*Vignettes*: (*a*) Ani adoring the Sun-god in his Bark. (*b*) Ani and his wife Tutu. Chapter 15 (continued), including hymn to Ra, and litany to Osiris.

THE BOOK OF THE DEAD

CHAP. XV

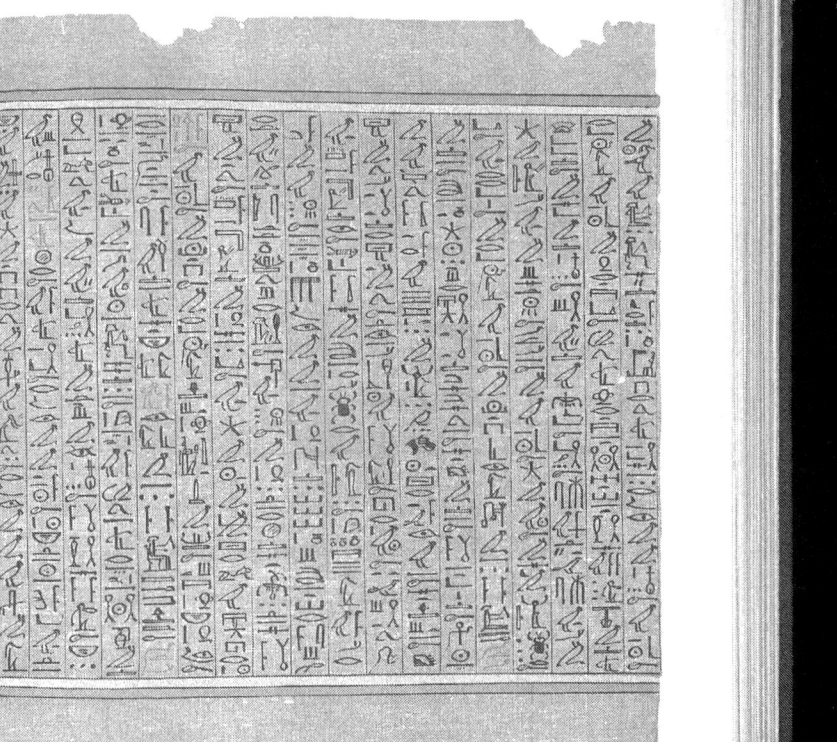

22.—*Vignette*: Osiris, with the sceptre, flail, and hook, and Isis, within a shrine.
Text: Chapter 15 of the Book of the Dead, (continued): Hymn to the Sun-god.

THE BOOK OF THE DEAD

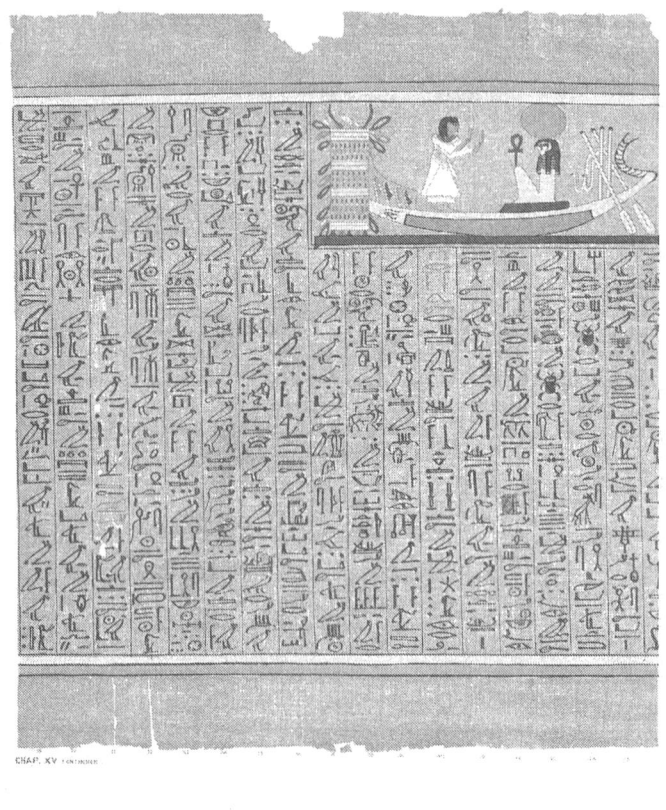

CHAP. XV (CONTINUED)

THE PAPYRUS OF ANI

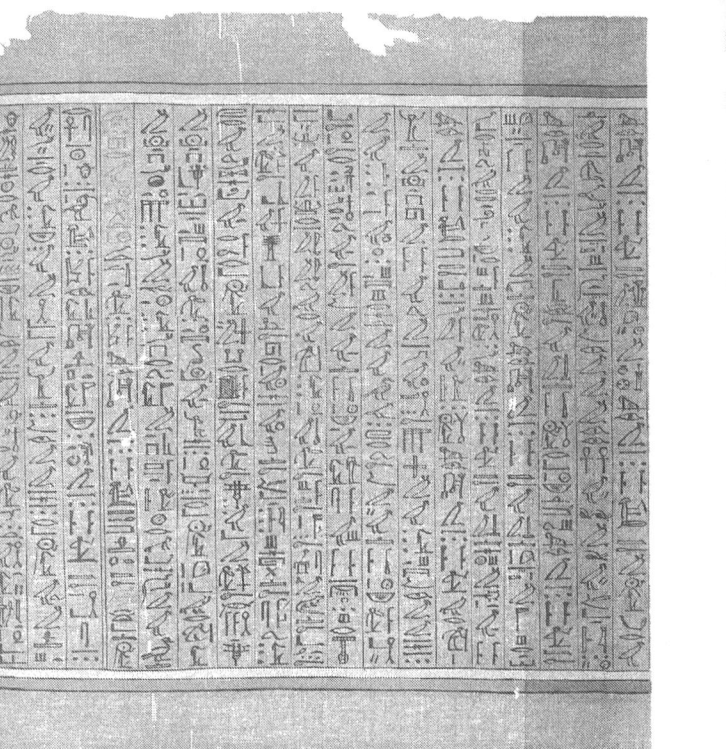

11.—*Vignette*: Ani in the Solar Bark, adoring the Sun-god.
Text: Chapters 15 (continuation) and 133 of the Book of the Dead, containing hymns to the Sun-god.

THE BOOK OF THE DEAD

THE PAPYRUS OF ANI

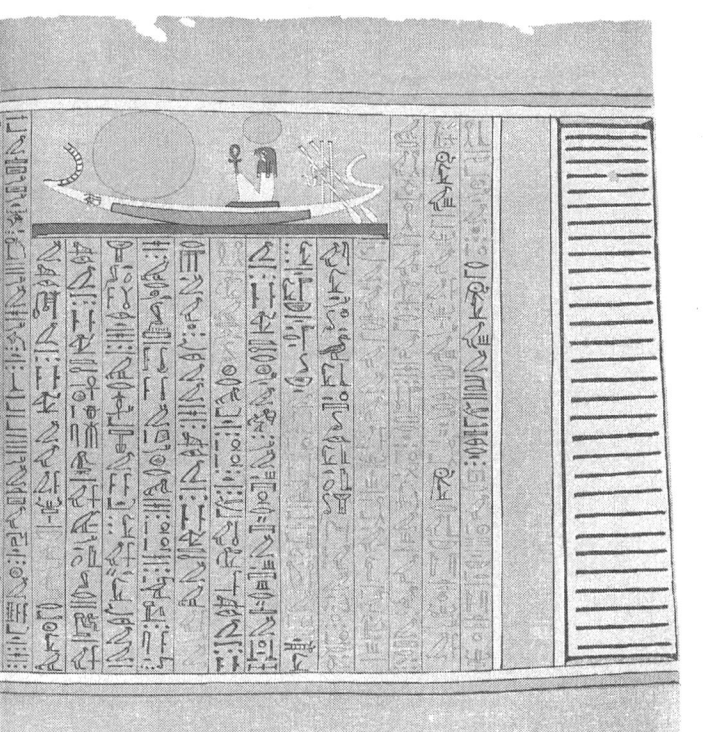

22.—*Vignettes*: The Sun-god in his Bark.
Text: Chapters 133 (continued) and 134 of the Book of the Dead.
At the end of the Plate is the ladder or flight of steps by which the soul mounts to visit the body in the tomb.

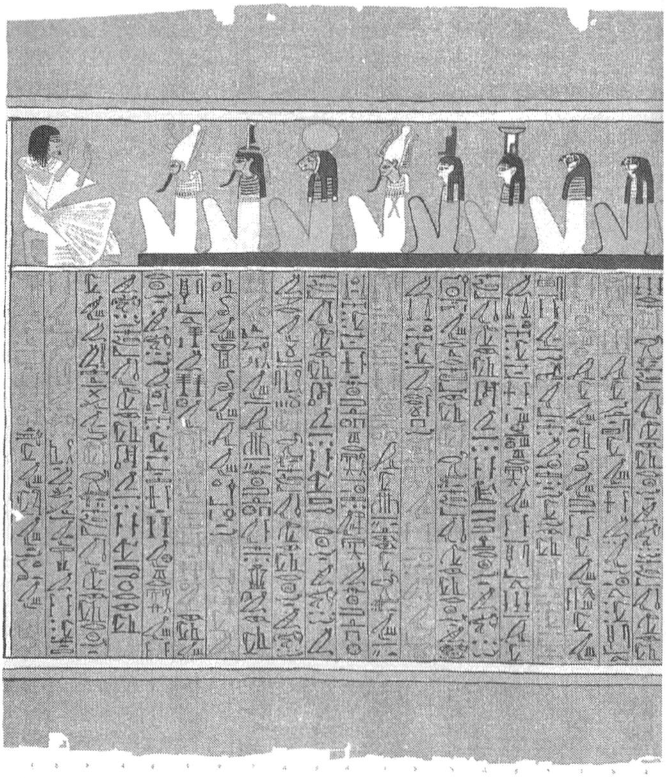

THE BOOK OF THE DEAD

A   B   C   D
CHAP XVIII

THE PAPYRUS OF ANI

23

13.—*Vignette*: Ani adoring the Powers of Localities, twenty of whom are here depicted (see Plates 13-14).
Text: Chapter 18 (repeated) of the Book of the Dead.

THE BOOK OF THE DEAD

THE PAPYRUS OF ANI

24

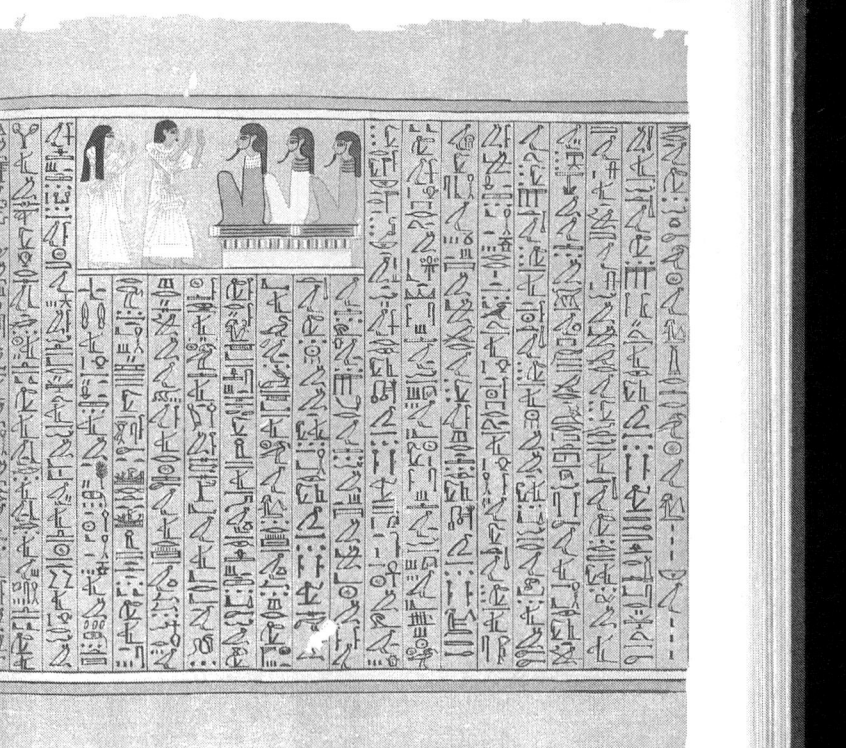

24.—*Vignettes*: (a) Eleven of the Powers of Locations (continued from Plate 23). (b) Ani and his wife adoring a triad of gods.
Text: Chapters 18 (continued) and 124 of the Book of the Dead; the latter describing the deceased's triumphant progress and state of bliss.

THE BOOK OF THE DEAD

CHAP. LXXXVI   CHAP. LXXXVII

THE PAPYRUS OF ANI

25

CHAP. LXXVIII.

75.—*Vignettes*: The Dove, the Golden Hawk, and the Divine Hawk, illustrating the chapters of the transformation of the deceased into three mythical forms of the Sun-god.
Text: Chapters of transformation, 76, 86, 77 and 78 of the Book of the Dead.

THE BOOK OF THE DEAD

CHAP. LXXVIII continued.

THE PAPYRUS OF ANI 26

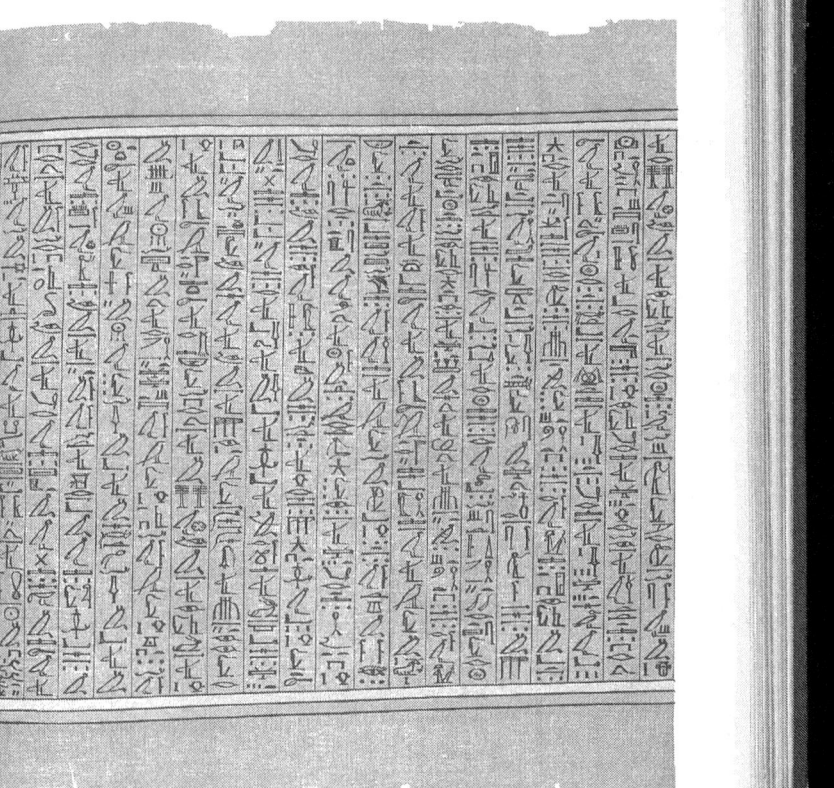

Chapter 78 (continued) of the Book of the Dead.

THE BOOK OF THE DEAD

CHAP. LXXXVII. CHAP. LXXXVIII. CHAP. LXXXIX.

THE PAPYRUS OF ANI 27

CHAP. LXXXV.   CHAP. LXXXIII.

17.—Vignettes: The Serpent Sa-ta, the Crocodile Sebak, the god Ptah, the Ram (soul of Tmu), and the Heron, illustrating transformations (continued from Plates 25 and 26).
Text: Chapters of transformation, viz., 87, 38, 82, 85, and 83 of the Book of the Dead.

THE BOOK OF THE DEAD

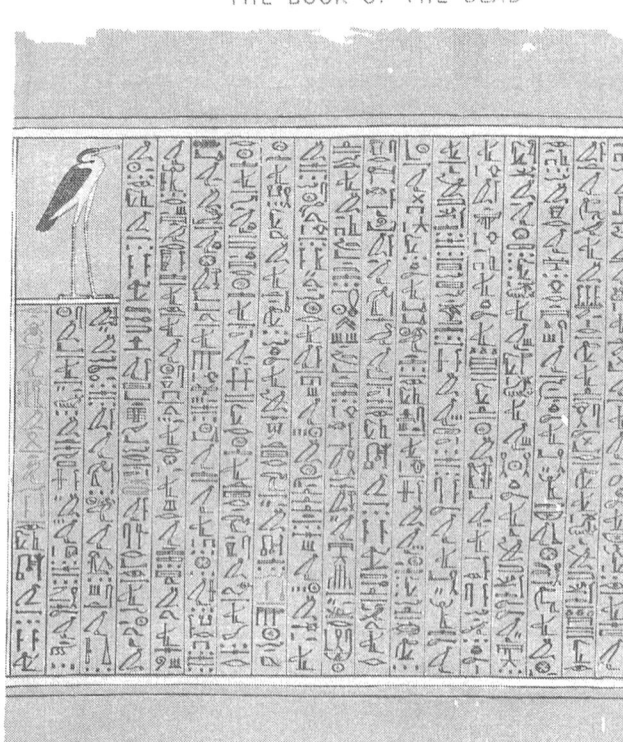

CHAP. LXXXIV.

THE PAPYRUS OF ANI

28

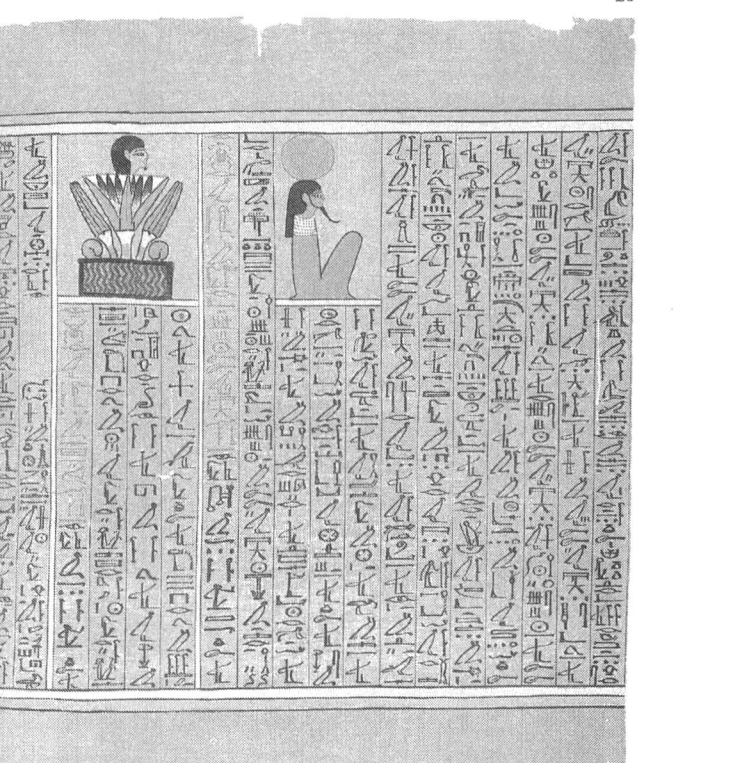

CHAP. LXXXI A.   CHAP. LXXX.

28.—*Vignettes*: Tem-Osiris, the Lotus, and the god who lightens the Darkness, illustrating transformations (reproduced from Plates 27-28).

Text: Chapters of transformation, viz., 84, 81A, and 80 of the Book of the Dead.

THE BOOK OF THE DEAD

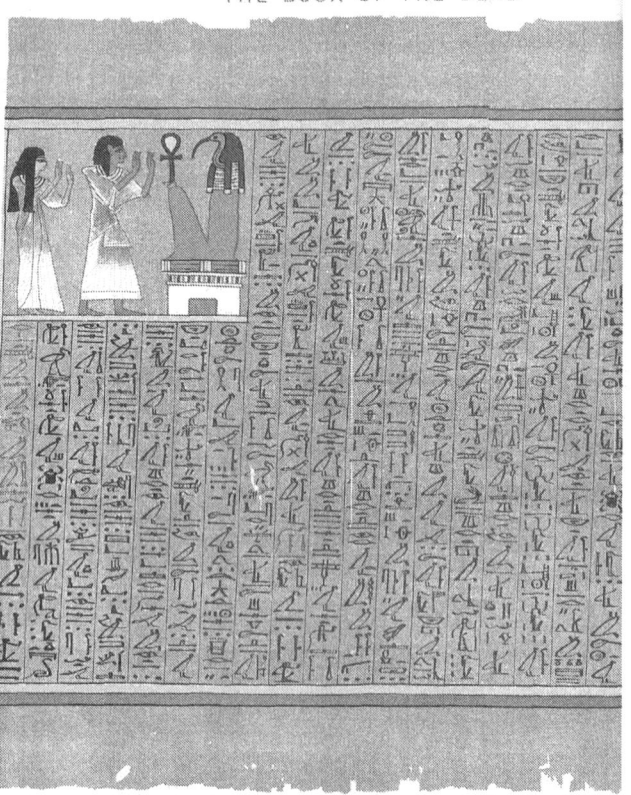

CHAP. CLXXV

10.—*Vignettes*: (a) Ani and his wife adoring Thoth. (b) Ani and his wife before a table of offerings.
Text: Chapter 175 of the Book of the Dead; and the latter portion of a new chapter which begins in Plate 30.

THE BOOK OF THE DEAD

CHAP. CXXV

THE PAPYRUS OF ANI

Vignette: Osiris and Isis within a shrine; before them a lotus-flower on which stand the four children of Horus, genii of the dead.
Text: An introductory chapter to the Negative Confession.

THE BOOK OF THE DEAD

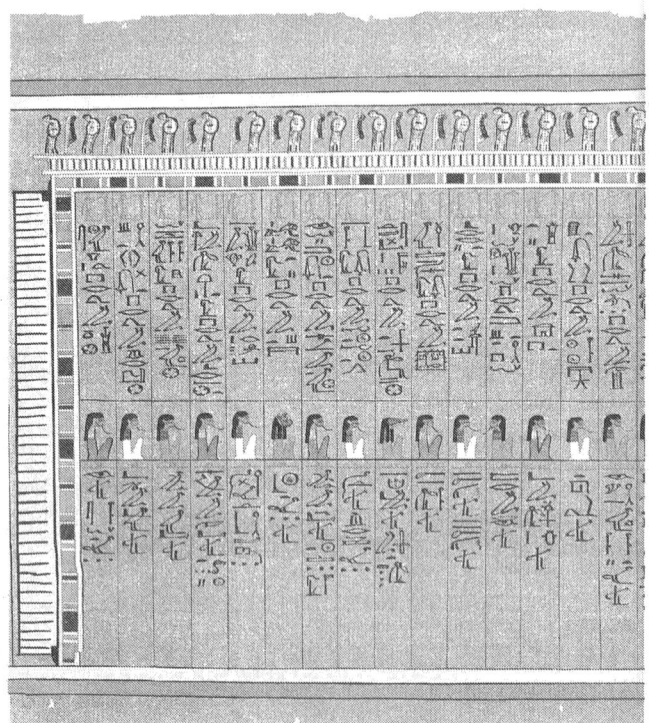

CHAP. CXXV. THE NEGATIVE CONFESSION.

THE PAPYRUS OF ANI

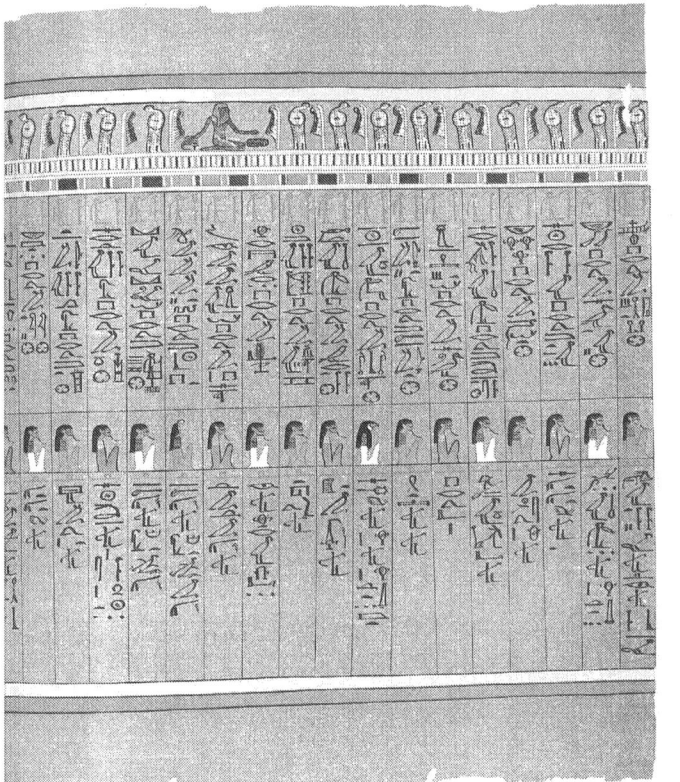

31.—*Vignette*: The Hall of the Two-fold Maat (part in Plate 32), decorated with uraei and feathers symbolical of Law (Maat). Within are the forty-two judges of the dead, thirty-three of whom are here depicted.
Text: Chapter 125 (the Negative Confession) of the Book of the Dead.

THE BOOK OF THE DEAD

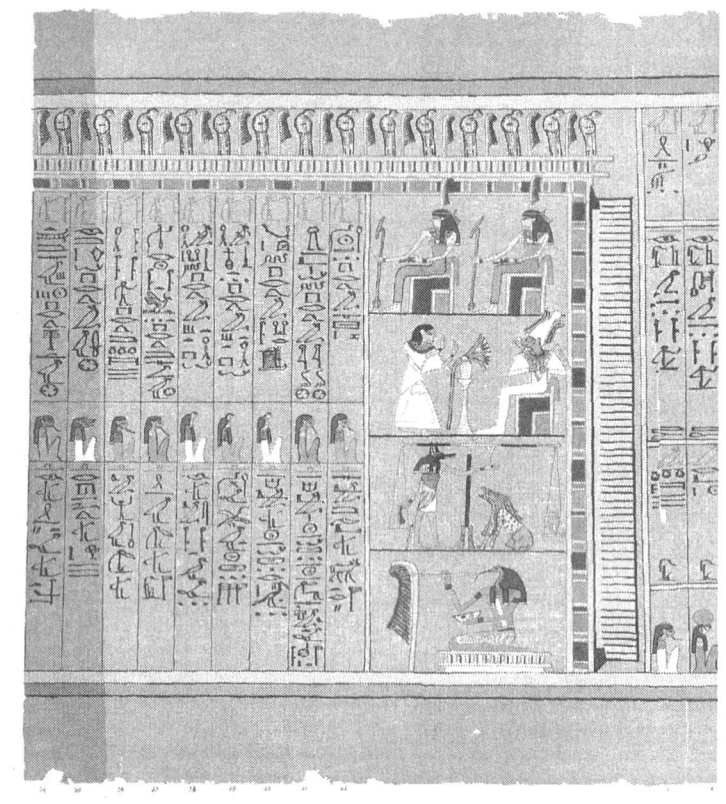

CHAP. CXXV. continued.   THE NEGATIVE CONFESSION   CHAP. XLII.

THE PAPYRUS OF ANI 32

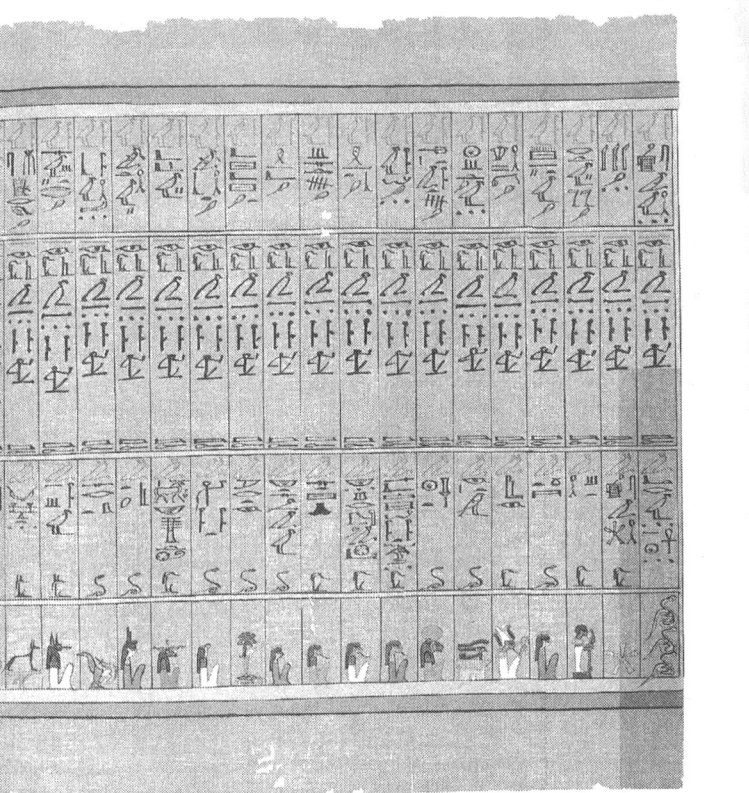

31.—Vignettes. (a) The Hall of the Two-fold Maāt (continued from Plate 31) showing the rest of the judges of the dead and, in four compartments, the two goddesses of Law, Ani adoring Osiris, the Trial of the Conscience (see Plate 3) and Thoth and the Feather of Law. (b) The twenty-three gods to whom are severally assigned various parts of the body.

Text. Chapters 125 (continued) and part of 42 (the Assimilation of Limbs) of the Book of the Dead.

THE BOOK OF THE DEAD

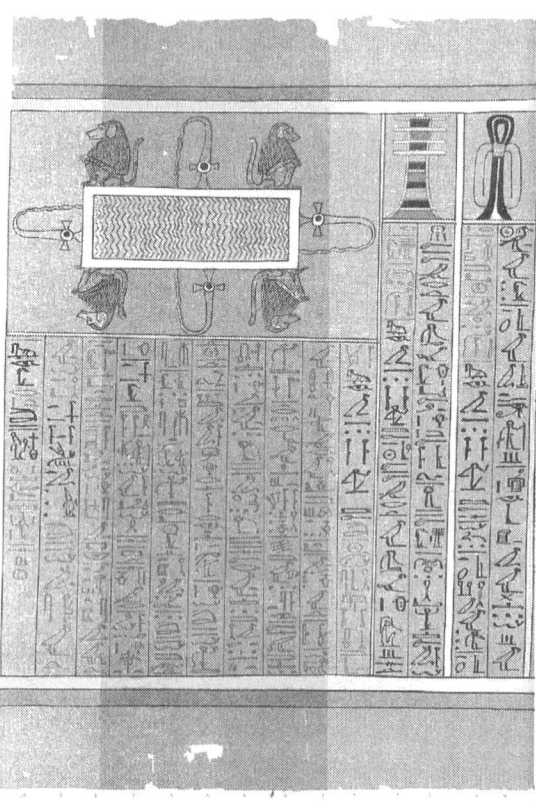

CHAP. XLII RUBRIC.   CHAP. CLV.   CHAP. CLVI

THE PAPYRUS OF ANI

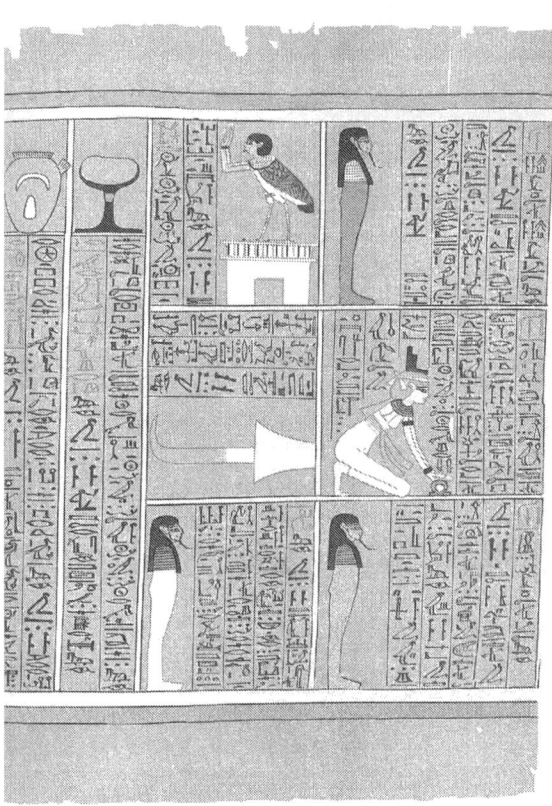

XXIX B. CHAP. CLXVI.   CHAP. CLI.

33.—*Vignettes.* (a) Four cynocephali, seated at the corners of a pool of fire, from which rise four flames. (b) The Tat, the Buckle, the Heart, and the Head-rest, four amulets placed upon the mummy. (c) Portion of the scene of the sepulchral chamber (see Plate 34).

Text: Rubric of chapter 42 (Rotate), and chapters 155, 156, 166, and 151 of the Book of the Dead.

THE BOOK OF THE DEAD

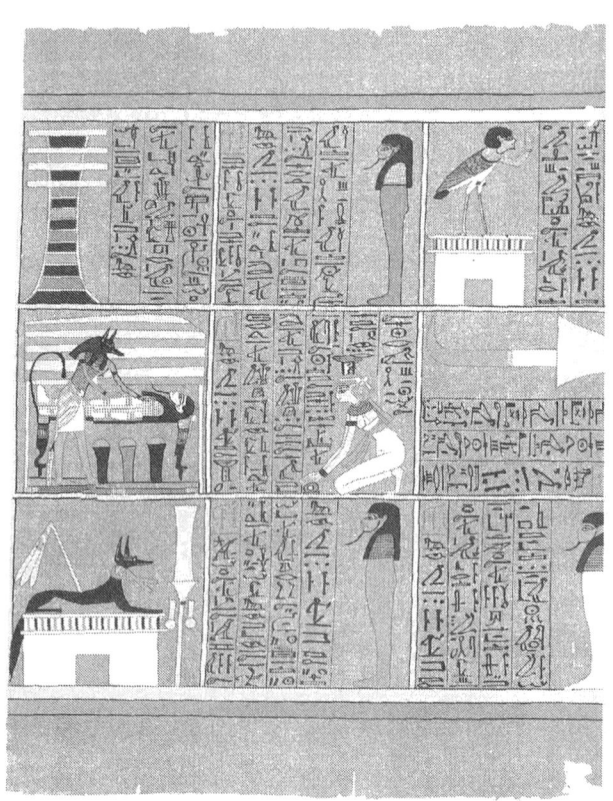

CHAP. CLI.

THE PAPYRUS OF ANI

34.—*Vignettes*: (a) Scene of the sepulchral chamber: the mummy on its bier, guarded by Anubis; Isis (Plate 33) kneeling at the foot, and Nephthys at the head; at the four corners, the four children of Horus; above, the Tat; below, Ap-uat on a tomb; on the extreme right and left, in three compartments, the soul, a flame of fire, and a Shabtu figure designed to assist the deceased in the labours of the nether-world. (b) Ani and his wife before a table of offerings.

Text: Chapters 151 (continued) and 110 (description of the Elysian Fields) of the Book of the Dead.

THE BOOK OF THE DEAD

CHAP CX. VIGNETTE.

THE PAPYRUS OF ANI

CHAP. CXLVIII.

35.—*Vignettes.* (a) The occupations of Ani in the Elysian Fields, through which flow rivers of water. Thoth first introducing the deceased and his Shaï(?) into the presence of a triad of gods. (b) A Hall (part of Plate 36?) in which Ani adores Ra, before two altars with vases and lotus flowers, and the seven Cows and the Bull provide food for him. *Text (Chapters 110: Vignette) and 148.*

THE BOOK OF THE DEAD

CHAP. CXLVIII.

THE PAPYRUS OF ANI

ADORATION OF OSIRIS

Vignettes: (a) The Hall (continued from Plate 33), in which are the four Rudders of Heaven and four triads of gods. (b) Ani and his wife before a table of offerings.
Text: Chapters 148 and 185 (adoration of Osiris) of the Book of the Dead.

THE BOOK OF THE DEAD

CHAP. CLXXXVI.

THE PAPYRUS OF ANI

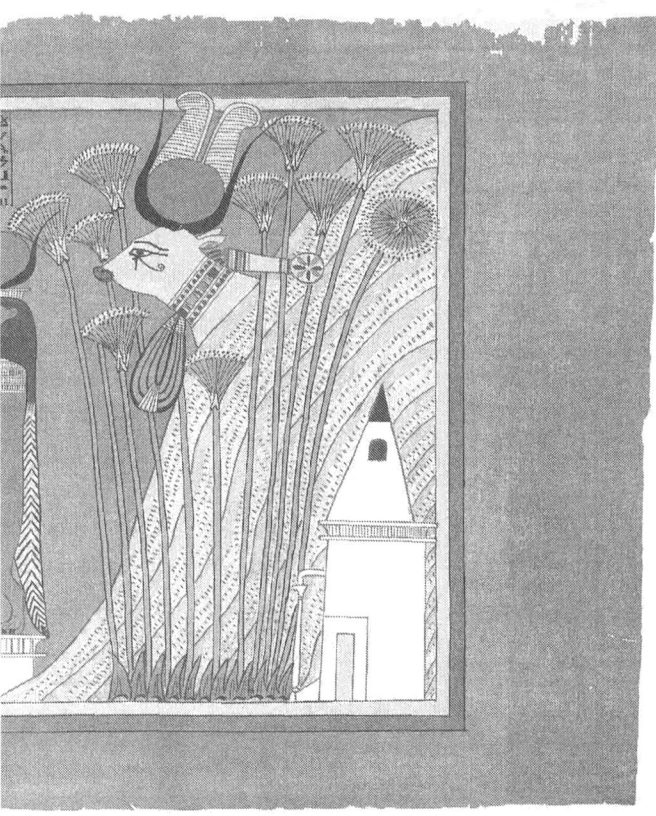

37.—*Vignettes*: (a) Osiris-Sokar within a shrine (adored by Ani and his wife, Plate 36). (b) The goddess Hathor, as a hippopotamus, crowned with the sun-disk and horns; before her, a table of offerings; behind, the Meh-urit Cow, symbolizing the same goddess, who gazes forth from the mountain of Amenta, at the foot of which is the tomb.

Text: Chapters 148 and 186 of the Book of the Dead.

Ingram Content Group UK Ltd.
Milton Keynes UK
UKHW021255260723
425816UK00016B/419